Cranbury Public Library

23 North Main St., Cranbury, NJ 08512
(609) 655-0555   f: (609) 655-2858

www.CranburyPublicLibrary.org

D1539772

Cookies

by **Dana Meachen Rau**

Reading Consultant: Nanci R. Vargus, Ed.D.

Marshall Cavendish
Benchmark
New York

Picture Words

 chocolate chips

 cookie

 cookie jar

 cookies

 peanuts

 plate

 stars

We eat 🍪 after lunch.

We eat 🍪.

Crunch, crunch!

 can be full of .

A 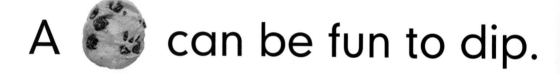 can be fun to dip.

 can have .

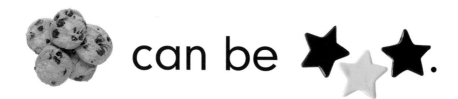 can be ★★.

 can have sugar.

 can fill up a .

There are many .

I cannot wait!

The  are all gone.

I have an empty .

Words to Know

dip   to put into

crunch (krunch)
    to chew

empty (EMP-tee)
    nothing in or on

Find Out More

Books

Dunnington, Rose. *The Greatest Cookies Ever: Dozens of Delicious, Chewy, Chunky, Fun and Foolproof Recipes.* New York: Lark Books, 2005.

Lin, Grace. *Fortune Cookie Fortunes.* New York: Dragonfly Books, 2006.

Wellington, Monica. *Mr. Cookie Baker.* New York: Dutton Children's Books, 2006.

Videos

Kid Vids Educational Entertainment. *Show and Tell: Milk and Cookies.* Chicago, IL: MPI Home Video.

GBC. *Gingerbread Fun for Everyone.* Crofton, MD.

Web Sites

The History of Chocolate Chip Cookies
www.extremechocolate.com/historyofchocolate chipcookies.html

USDA: MyPyramid.gov
www.mypyramid.gov/kids/index.html

About the Author

Dana Meachen Rau is an author, editor, and illustrator. A graduate of Trinity College in Hartford, Connecticut, she has written more than two hundred books for children, including nonfiction, biographies, early readers, and historical fiction. She likes to bake cookies with her family in Burlington, Connecticut.

About the Reading Consultant

Nanci R. Vargus, Ed.D., wants all children to enjoy reading. She used to teach first grade. Now she works at the University of Indianapolis. Nanci helps young people become teachers. She likes to decorate cookies with her granddaughters Charlotte, Corinne, and AJ.

Marshall Cavendish Benchmark
99 White Plains Road
Tarrytown, NY 10591-5502
www.marshallcavendish.us

Copyright © 2009 by Marshall Cavendish Corporation

All Internet sites were correct at the time of printing.

Library of Congress Cataloging-in-Publication Data
Rau, Dana Meachen, 1971–
Cookies / by Dana Meachen Rau
     p. cm. — (Benchmark rebus. What's Cooking?)
Summary: "Easy to read text with rebuses explores different varieties of cookies"—Provided by Publisher.
Includes bibliographical references.
ISBN 978-0-7614-2890-9 (alk. paper)
Cookies—Juvenile literature. I. Title.
TX772.R38 2009
641.8'654—dc22
     2007021283

Editor: Christine Florie
Publisher: Michelle Bisson
Art Director: Anahid Hamparian
Series Designer: Virginia Pope

Photo research by Connie Gardner

Rebus images provided courtesy of *Dorling Kindersley.*

Cover photo by *Somos/Veer/Getty Images*

The photographs in this book are used with permission and through the courtesy of:
The Image Works: p. 5 Bob Daemmrich; *Jupiter Images*: pp. 7, 13, 15, 17 FoodPix; *SuperStock*: p. 9 Nathan Michaels; p. 19 age footstock; *Getty Images*: p. 11 Renee Comet; *PhotoEdit*: p. 21 Michael Newman.

Printed in Malaysia
1 3 5 6 4 2

DATE DUE

Cake

by **Dana Meachen Rau**

Reading Consultant: Nanci R. Vargus, Ed.D.

Marshall Cavendish
Benchmark
New York

Picture Words

 apron

 cake

 candles

 flowers

 sprinkles

 strawberries

3

It is party time.

We need a .

Grab an .

Bake a !

A can have .

A can be tall.

A  can have .

A can be small.

Add some 🍓🍓.

Put your on a dish.

Blow out the |||||||.

Make a wish!

Words to Know

apron (AY-pruhn)
a piece of clothing you wear
over your clothes to keep
yourself clean

dish a plate used to hold food

sprinkles (SPRING-kuhls)
tiny bits of candy

wish something wanted or hoped for

Find Out More

Books

Brenn-White, Megan. *Bake Me a Cake: Fun and Easy Treats for Kids*. New York: Harper Resource, 2005.

Frasier, Debra. *A Birthday Cake Is No Ordinary Cake*. Orlando, FL: Harcourt Children's Books, 2006.

Smith, Lindy. *Party Animal Cakes*. Cincinnati, OH: F & W Publications, Inc., 2006.

Videos

Salter Street Films. *Fantastic Foods*. Sony Wonder.

Web Sites

Easy Kids Recipes: Birthday Party Cakes
www.easy-kids-recipes.com/birthday-party- cakes.html

FamilyFun.com: Cakes and Cupcakes
familyfun.go.com/recipes/special/minisite2/cakes_and_ cupcakes

USDA: MyPyramid.gov
www.mypyramid.gov/kids/index.html

About the Author

Dana Meachen Rau is an author, editor, and illustrator. A graduate of Trinity College in Hartford, Connecticut, she has written more than two hundred books for children, including nonfiction, biographies, early readers, and historical fiction. She likes to make cakes with her family in Burlington, Connecticut.

About the Reading Consultant

Nanci R. Vargus, Ed.D., wants all children to enjoy reading. She used to teach first grade. Now she works at the University of Indianapolis. Nanci helps young people become teachers. Her favorite kind of cake is carrot cake.

Marshall Cavendish Benchmark
99 White Plains Road
Tarrytown, NY 10591-5502
www.marshallcavendish.us

All Internet addresses were correct at the time of printing.

Library of Congress Cataloging-In-Publication Data
Rau, Dana Meachen, 1971–
Cake / by Dana Meachen Rau
    p. cm. — (Benchmark Rebus : What's Cooking?)
Summary: "Easy to read text with rebuses explores the different varieties of cake"—Provided by publisher.
Includes bibliographical references.
ISBN 978-0-7614-2896-1
1. Cake — Juvenile literature. I. Title.
TX771.R385 2008
641.8'653—dc22
2007023832

Editor: Christine Florie
Publisher: Michelle Bisson
Art Director: Anahid Hamparian
Series Designer: Virginia Pope

Photo research by Connie Gardner

Rebus images provided courtesy of *Dorling Kindersley.*

Cover photo by SuperStock/Stockbyte

SuperStock: age footstock, 9, 21; *Getty Images*: Jake Fitzjones, 7; Matilida Lindebald, 17; *PhotoEdit*: Spencer Grant, 11; *Corbis*: Richard Hutchings, 5; Envisions, 13; *Jupiter Images*: Kathryn Russell, 15; Foodpix, 19.

Printed in Malaysia
1 3 5 6 4 2